GW01326473

THUNDER BOX

BOVINGTON MIDDLE SCHOOL
LIBRARY

THUNDER BOX

Heather Hammonds

Nelson

an International Thomson Publishing company I(T)P®

Melbourne • Albany, NY • Belmont, CA • Boston • Cincinnati • Johannesburg
London • Madrid • Mexico City • New York • Pacific Grove, CA
Scottsdale, AZ • Singapore • Tokyo • Toronto

Nelson I(T)P®
102 Dodds Street
South Melbourne 3205

Email nelsonitp@nelson.com.au
Website http://www.nelsonitp.com

Nelson I(T)P® *an International Thomson Publishing company*

First published in 2000
10 9 8 7 6 5 4 3 2 1
08 07 06 05 04 03 02 01 00

Copyright © Nelson ITP, 2000

COPYRIGHT
Apart from fair dealing for the purposes of study, research, criticism or
review, or as permitted under Part VB of the Copyright Act, no part of
this book may be reproduced by any process without permission.
Copyright owners may take legal action against a person who infringes
on their copyright through unauthorised copying. Enquiries should be
directed to the publisher.

National Library of Australia
Cataloguing-in-Publication data

Hammonds, Heather.
    Thunder Box.
    ISBN 017 010164 9.
    ISBN 017 010162 2 (set).
    I. Title. (Series: BlitzIt).
    A823.3

Edited by Carmel Heron
Illustrated by Rupert Freeman
Cover designed by Christine Deering
Text designed by Christine Deering
Typeset in Clearface by J&M Typesetters
Printed in Singapore by Kin Keong Printing Co. Pte Ltd

Nelson Australia Pty Limited ACN 058 280 149 (incorporated in
Victoria) trading as Nelson ITP.

Contents

Chapter 1

Grandpa Bill's

"Yippee, we're here," Rod shouted, startling Sean who had been dozing in the back seat.

Sean rubbed his eyes and stared out of the window at the funniest little farmhouse he had ever seen. It sat right near the top of a steep, grassy hill and its rusty iron roof sagged in the middle, making it look old and tired.

Rod's grandpa had invited the two boys to stay for a week at his farm during their school holidays and, at first, Sean had been keen to go. Now he wasn't so sure. What were they going to do all the way out here in the middle of nowhere for a whole week? No TV, no computer games, no park to play in – it could turn out to be really boring. Still, Rod seemed excited enough for both of them.

"There's Grandpa Bill – he must have heard the car," said Rod.

Rod's dad was steering the car up the long gravel driveway to the farmhouse. A tall, thin man, with grey hair and a pointy nose like Rod's dad's, was smiling and waving to the boys.

"Grandpa Bill," Rod yelled, jumping out of the car as soon as they pulled up, and giving the old man a hug. "This is my friend, Sean."

"Hello, lad," said Grandpa Bill, giving Sean's hand a hearty shake. "Pleased to meet you."

Rod and Sean took their stuff out of the car boot while Rod's dad talked to Grandpa Bill.

"Where are we sleeping?" asked Sean,

staring doubtfully at the house, which looked even more in need of repair now that they were standing right next to it.

Rod led Sean around the back of the house to an enclosed veranda. Inside, it smelt of damp wood and mothballs. Sean wrinkled his nose. They threw their sleeping bags down on two foam mattresses that Grandpa Bill had laid out for them, and put the rest of their belongings in a big wooden wardrobe that leaned against one wall.

"This place is great," Rod sighed. "Grandpa never gets mad if you bring in mud on your shoes, or forget to tidy your bed, or leave crumbs on the kitchen table. He's really relaxed about that sort of thing. I suppose it's because he lives on his own now, since Grandma died."

"Yeah," said Sean, looking around. "It doesn't look like he worries much about cleaning up."

"Well, why would he?" asked Rod, annoyed

that Sean had agreed with him. "Grandpa has so many fun things to do here that he doesn't get time to clean up. He has his own cow to milk, some chickens and a rooster, and a whole flock of sheep to look after. Sometimes he goes fishing in the river at the bottom of the paddock. And if he ever gets bored, he can go down to the holiday camp over the other side of the hill and talk to the people there."

"You're right. Who would want to waste time cleaning up, anyway?" replied Sean, wondering how Rod could think those things were exciting, but not wanting to annoy him further by saying so.

The boys went back outside to wave goodbye to Rod's dad, because he was ready to drive back home. As the car disappeared up the road, Sean knew that now he was definitely stuck at the farm – for a whole week.

"Do you feel like some lunch now, boys?" asked Grandpa Bill.

"Thanks Grandpa, but first I'm going to use the thunder box. I'd better show Sean where it is, too," answered Rod.

Grandpa Bill and Rod laughed at the puzzled look on Sean's face.

"Thunder box?" he asked. "What's a thunder box?"

"It's the toilet," laughed Rod. "Out here, most people have outdoor toilets away from the house, because there's no sewerage. They're usually called thunder boxes."

"And this one really *is* a thunder box," added Grandpa Bill. "It had a bit of an accident the other night when there was a big storm; we've been getting a lot of thunder and lightning out here lately."

"What happened to it, Grandpa?" asked Rod.

The old man smiled and shook his head. "It was amazing! A big bolt of lightning hit the pine tree just behind the thunder box. It burnt a couple of branches right off it. I happened to be looking out of the kitchen window at the time and saw the whole thing. The lightning ran right down the tree and into the thunder box, making it glow bright blue for a second. It blew a little hole in the roof and then that was that. Lucky nobody was sitting in there at the time…"

"Wow," chuckled Rod.

"That could have been dangerous," said Sean.

"Like I said, now it really is a genuine thunder box," laughed Grandpa Bill.

Sean followed Rod around the back of the house again and along a little path through long grass. Not far down the path stood a small square building with a wooden door that hung loosely on its hinges. Behind it was the pine tree with two of its branches lying on the ground, broken and burnt.

"This is it," said Rod. "Wait here for me."

He disappeared inside and shut the door.

Sean tried to imagine himself coming out here in the middle of the night to go to the toilet. What if he stepped on a snake, or there was a spider on the toilet seat? Hadn't he heard a song about that somewhere? Oh, no…a whole week of using this thing. It was like living in the dark ages. Well, if there was no other toilet, he supposed he would have to grin and bear it, but definitely not during a thunderstorm!

Chapter 2

Take-off

Rod's grandpa had made a great lunch for the boys. There were hard-boiled eggs, lots of bread and jam, and some blackberries from a patch of brambles near the river. Sean and Rod ate as much as they could fit in. After they had finished, they went outside and climbed up the hill to a flat spot behind the farmhouse to kick a football around. Finally, Sean could put it off no longer. He had to use the thunder box.

"I'll be back in a minute," he called to Rod.

Down the path he went, staring hard at the rickety wooden door. It swung back and forth in the breeze, creaking eerily, as if inviting him in. Nervously, he pushed it open and stepped inside the small dark space. Sean closed the door behind him and locked it with a rusty old bolt so that it stayed shut. The thunder box smelt funny, and he noticed that there were cobwebs hanging off the toilet roll holder. The toilet seat was wooden, and it looked like you might get a splinter if you sat down too hard. Sean peered up at a small hole, with black burn marks around its edges, in one corner of the roof. He thought about the lightning Grandpa Bill had talked about that had caused the hole, and a shiver went up his spine.

"I hate this place," he grumbled to himself. "Why couldn't Rod and I have stayed at home this week and gone to the movies instead?"

Sean did what he had to do and turned around to leave, but as he put his hand on the bolt to let himself out, something weird happened. A bright blue light began to glow around the hole in the roof and he felt the whole thunder box move. The glow grew brighter, crackling and sizzling around the walls.

"Hey!" he called out. "What's going on?"

Sean waited as the thunder box rocked about and the blue light kept shining. He was really scared, but he tried not to scream or cry. Finally, the rocking stopped and the light disappeared, so he opened the door and peeked out.

"Oh, no," he whispered, slamming it shut again.

Outside, instead of a grassy path, there was a modern, carpeted hallway.

"This can't be happening," Sean told himself. "I must be imagining it."

Cautiously, he opened the door again, but the scene was the same. He looked in amazement. The outside of the door was brand new and painted with a sign that said 'Toilet'. The inside of the door was made of old wood – it was the thunder box.

Where am I? wondered Sean, feeling a fresh wave of panic rise in his stomach.

He knew that he couldn't stay in the toilet all day. He would have to go out and see what had happened.

Sean sneaked out of the thunder box and down the hallway. He could hear voices nearby and he followed them until he came to the door of an office. He stood there for a moment, listening to what was being said inside. The more Sean heard, the more worried he felt.

"We both know that the farm on the hill would be the perfect site, Mr Richardson," said a deep voice. "But the stupid old fogey who owns it doesn't want to sell it to me. I've tried my best to persuade him, but I can't make him change his mind. Isn't there *something* the council can do? Some way you can force him to sell the place? Think of how much tourism my holiday camp brings to the area. I could make the camp so much bigger ... "

"Sadly, the council can't help you," sighed a second voice. "But, if that old farmhouse were to burn down, somehow ... "

The first voice laughed nastily. "Yeah. Being such an old man, he probably wouldn't want to stay there any more. Besides, he might even have a heart attack and kick the bucket because of it. Then he wouldn't be around to bother us."

"Be careful," said the second voice. "And remember, if you get caught, you're on your own. We never had this conversation."

Sean held his breath and tiptoed quickly back to the toilet. This must be the local council office! And whoever those two men were, Sean was sure that they had been talking about Grandpa Bill's farm. Burn it down? Just to get the land for a holiday camp? Those men were crooks! He slipped back inside the thunder box and locked the door. Somehow, he had to get back to the farm. Carefully sitting down on the wooden seat, he put his chin in his hands and tried to think.

Just then, the blue light glowed around the hole again and the thunder box began to rattle.

"Please take me back to the farm now," whispered Sean. "I've got to tell Rod!"

Chapter 3

Aliens!

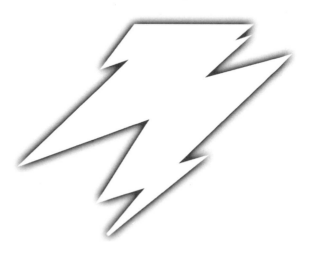

While Rod was waiting for Sean to go to the toilet, he kicked the football around by himself. Dark clouds began to float across the sky and, in the distance, he heard a rumble of thunder. He hoped it wasn't going to rain.

After a while, Rod started to get bored. Why was Sean taking so long? He decided to go and investigate. Walking down to the back of the farmhouse he called out, "Sean! Are you still in there? Have you fallen in or got stuck?"

There was no answer from the thunder box at first and then, slowly, the door opened. A white-faced Sean poked his head outside and looked around.

"Am I glad to see you," he gasped. "You won't believe what just happened!"

Rod put his hands on his hips and shook his head.

"Okay, perhaps you did nearly fall in. Or did you get a splinter? Come on, let's get on with our game!" He turned around and began to walk away, expecting Sean to follow him.

"Wait!" Sean cried out, running up and grabbing Rod by the arm. "This is important! It's about your grandpa's house. The thunder box ... *that* thunder box is no ordinary toilet. I found out something while I was in there. I think the farmhouse is in danger!"

"What are you talking about?" Rod asked. "I've used that thunder box for years and there's nothing special about it."

15

"Well, there is now," insisted Sean. "Let me explain … "

Sean quickly told Rod all that had happened to him when he'd gone to the toilet. Rod didn't exactly laugh at him, but Sean could tell that his friend didn't believe what he'd said.

"No offence, but I think you must have fallen asleep in there and dreamt all of that," said Rod when Sean had finished his story.

"You don't think that it happened?" asked Sean, trying not to get annoyed. After all, he could hardly believe it himself.

Rod shrugged his shoulders and looked at the cloudy sky. "I don't know. Look, next time you need to go, I'll come with you and we'll see if anything strange happens again. In the meantime, let's get on with our game before it starts to rain."

The boys made their way back to the flat grassy spot. Rod kicked the ball to Sean, but Sean just stood there, looking up at the sky.

"What's the matter now?" Rod called out.

"Aliens," he said.

"What?" asked Rod.

"Aliens," repeated Sean. "I saw something on television, on one of those 'unexplained happenings' shows, about someone being taken away by aliens. Maybe that's what happened to me when I was in the thunder box."

Rod shook his head and sighed. "No way! Most of what they say on those shows is completely made up. Aliens didn't abduct you."

"Oh, really?" Sean said, with his hands on his hips. "Well, I think that they might have."

"You mean you actually think that my grandpa's thunder box was abducted by aliens, with you inside it?" asked Rod, falling down and rolling around on the grass, helpless with laughter. "Why would they bother? It's falling apart! I'm sure they'd have toilets on their space ships. They wouldn't need to steal ours."

"Very funny," replied Sean grumpily. "Well, you asked what I thought and that's what I think. And if you listened to what I told you before, you would know that we'd better keep a close eye on your grandpa's house while we're here. Because somebody wants to burn it down, and they don't care if your grandpa gets hurt when they do it!"

The two boys walked back to Grandpa Bill's farmhouse in silence, furious with each other. Sean was angry because Rod wouldn't believe him about the thunder box and was making fun of his ideas about aliens. Rod was angry with Sean because he kept coming up with crazy ideas and interrupting their game of football.

"I'm going inside," said Rod with a scowl.

But just as he was about to walk off, Sean heard a familiar voice. "Listen!" he hissed.

Both boys could hear a deep voice coming from around the front of the house. A brand new four-wheel drive was parked in the driveway.

"That's Mr Evans, the owner of the holiday camp on the other side of the hill," said Rod. "He let me play on his basketball court when I stayed here last year."

"That's the man who was talking about trying to burn your grandpa's house down!" said Sean. "I'd recognise his voice anywhere."

Rod and Sean hurried over, their anger at each other forgotten.

"You can't blame me for asking you again, Bill," Mr Evans was saying, as he got into his car. "You've got a lovely view from this hilltop. Any time you want to sell, let me know first."

"Thank you, Wilbur, but, as I've said before, this land will be passed on to my sons when I die," replied Grandpa Bill.

With a cheery wave, Mr Evans drove away.

"Has he been trying to buy the farm?" asked Rod in a small voice.

"Yes," laughed Grandpa Bill. "He asks me every time I see him. Wants to extend his holiday camp over this way. You needn't worry though, Rod, because I'm not selling!"

Rod and Sean looked at each other. Sean raised his eyebrows, as if to say, "I told you so!"

Chapter 4

Spying on the Enemy

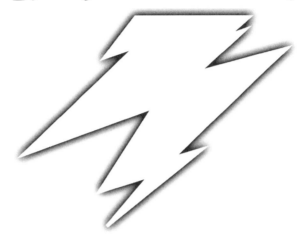

"I'm sorry, Sean. I should have believed you when you told me what happened in the thunder box," said Rod.

The two friends were sitting on the mattresses in their veranda room, eating ice-creams.

"That's okay," replied Sean, licking some sticky drops off his fingers. "I don't think I would have believed you either, if it had been your story. The main thing is, we've got to stop

Mr Evans from burning down the farmhouse. I think that's why they took me to the council office – so I would hear what was going on and we could do something about it."

"*They* took you to the council?" asked Rod. "*Who* do you think took you there?"

"The aliens, of course," replied Sean in a serious voice.

Rod sighed. "I told you before, Sean, it's not aliens. If aliens wanted to stop Mr Evans, they would just do it themselves. I'm sure he'd be more likely to listen to a bunch of aliens than a couple of kids. And anyway, why would aliens care who owns this farm?"

"I don't know," frowned Sean. "But I can't think of anything else that could make the thunder box do what it did. Can you?"

Rod was silent. The only idea he could come up with was that maybe the thunder box flew off on its own, and *that* was so crazy he didn't even want to mention it to Sean!

"No," he sighed. "But aliens or no aliens, we're still going to have to stop Mr Evans ourselves. First of all, we need to set a trap. If he's going to try to set fire to the house, we have to catch him right in the act, and get the police out here in time to arrest him."

"It would be nice to know exactly when he was going to come and do it," Sean said. "I wonder if the thunder box might help us again?"

The boys stared out of the veranda window at the thunder box, which was sitting quietly under the pine tree, just as it always did.

"It's probably no use, but we may as well go over there and try it out," said Rod.

There wasn't much room inside the thunder box for two people. Rod and Sean squeezed in and locked the door. Outside, the sun was shining and it was hot; inside, it was dank and dark, and the thunder box smelt pretty bad.

"What now?" asked Rod, holding his nose. "Do we have to say anything to make it go?"

"I don't know," said Sean. "I suppose we just wait and see what happens. Whatever – or whoever – made the thunder box go to the council office might know we need help again."

"Well, I'm not waiting in here long – it stinks too much," said Rod.

After a minute, Sean looked up at the hole in the roof and noticed that it was beginning to glow. The door creaked and the toilet gurgled.

"Did you hear that?" he asked.

Rod nodded. Suddenly, the thunder box began to shake, and blue light spread around the walls. Rod clung to the back of Sean's T-shirt in fright, but Sean wasn't scared because he had seen this happen before. The shaking stopped, more quickly this time.

"Well, we're here, wherever that is," said Sean. Slowly, he unbolted the door and the two boys peeked outside.

"I think we're at the holiday camp," said Rod. "Look! There's the basketball court I was telling you about."

Why have we been brought here? wondered Sean.

Then the boys saw Mr Evans coming out of a nearby shed. They quickly ducked back inside. He walked right past them, carrying a can of petrol over to his four-wheel drive. They could hear a lady's voice, shouting at him.

"That's his wife," whispered Rod.

"Wilbur!" yelled the woman. "I don't care what that fool at the council told you to do. Someone could get hurt!"

"Be quiet, Frances," said Mr Evans. "I'm setting fire to that house at midnight, whether you like it or not. The old geezer won't sell and I want that land. If he gets hurt, that's too bad. The firemen will probably just think a bolt of lightning struck the house, with all the storms we've had lately."

Rod was so angry that he wanted to jump out and hit Mr Evans, but Sean stopped him.

"Don't be silly," he warned. "We found out what we need to know. Now all we have to do is wait to be taken back to Grandpa Bill's. If you go out there now, you'll ruin everything."

Rod knew that Sean was right, so he locked the thunder box door and they waited quietly. Soon, the shaking began again and, in no time at all, they were back at the farmhouse.

Chapter 5

The Plan ...

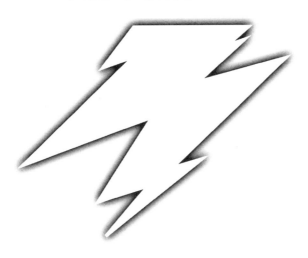

"Where have you been, boys?" called Grandpa Bill when he saw Rod and Sean walking back from the thunder box. "I've been looking for you for ages."

"Oh, just playing football," answered Rod. "But we lost our ball and had to go and look for it."

"Dear me," said Grandpa. "Well, never mind. Come in now, because I thought we could have a camp-fire tonight. You lads can light the fire, if you're careful."

All through their dinner by the camp-fire, Rod and Sean were very quiet as they both worked hard to try and think of a plan for capturing Mr Evans.

"Are you boys okay?" asked Grandpa Bill. "You don't seem to be having a very good time. I know I'm an old man and pretty boring, but I thought there would be plenty for you to see and do here on the farm."

"Oh, we're not bored, Grandpa," said Rod hastily. "We're just tired, aren't we Sean? I think we'd better have an early night tonight, that's all."

"Must be the country air," added Sean.

"Ah, yes," sighed Grandpa. "I remember when I was a young boy and I used to wear myself out, kicking a football and running around. Now I get tired doing nothing at all."

"Never mind, Grandpa," said Rod, giving him a big hug. "We really are having a great time. We love it here."

The two friends then said goodnight to Grandpa Bill and headed off to their beds inside the covered-in veranda.

"Thought of anything?" asked Sean, watching a little spider weave a web to trap flies, right in the corner of the window. The spider gave him an idea.

"No," sighed Rod, shaking his head glumly.

"Well … I sort of have a plan," said Sean slowly. "We'll need the thunder box again, and some strong rope. We can try to trap him inside it … "

He began to explain his idea to Rod.

• • •

The hours ticked by, and soon Grandpa Bill put the camp-fire out and headed for bed. The farmhouse was silent, except for the tin roof creaking in the night air and the distant rumble of thunder every now and again.

"Grandpa keeps ropes and a torch in his milking shed," whispered Rod, as the two boys sneaked out of the house and into the night.

"Now, remember what you said this afternoon," said Sean. "We have to catch Mr Evans right in the act. So, we must let him get the petrol out of his four-wheel drive and carry it over to the house, otherwise the police might not believe us when we explain what he was about to do."

"Okay," answered Rod. "But I'm worried, Sean. If the plan goes wrong, the house could be ruined."

Sean nodded. "That's why we have to make sure it doesn't go wrong."

The boys headed over to the old milking shed, feeling a bit scared. They could still hear thunder every now and again and see some flashes of lightning. A cold wind pulled at their clothes, making them shiver. Once they were inside the shed, Rod knew just where to find what they were looking for. Soon, the reassuring beam of a torch was lighting their way, as they carried a long coil of rope up to the thunder box.

"Listen!" hissed Sean.

The back door of the farmhouse banged and Grandpa Bill came walking slowly up the path with a newspaper tucked under his arm.

"Oh, no," whispered Rod. "Grandpa must be going to use the thunder box."

"Hope he isn't in there long," Sean muttered, looking at his watch. "It's half past eleven now. Mr Evans said he was going to come up here at midnight. We don't want him arriving before Grandpa Bill is safely out of the toilet and tucked up in bed asleep, or our plan will be ruined."

Bang! went the door of the old thunder box, as Grandpa went in and locked it. A minute later, a dim light shone through the cracks in the walls.

"He keeps a candle in there so he can read the paper at night," explained Rod.

There was nothing the boys could do but keep quiet and wait. After quite a few minutes, Grandpa Bill came back out again, folding the newspaper up. Sean let out a sigh of relief.

"Whew," he said when they heard the door of the farmhouse close. "I thought he'd never come out of there."

"Must have been reading the sports pages," said Rod.

They left the rope behind the thunder box and ran down the path to stand guard near the house and wait for Mr Evans. At two minutes to midnight, they heard a car engine. At the bottom of the gravel driveway, Mr Evans' four-wheel drive pulled up. Its lights were off, making it hard to see what he was up to. Rod and Sean heard gravel crunch, as Mr Evans went around to the back of the car and lifted out the can of petrol they had seen him put in there earlier.

Chapter 6

Trapped!

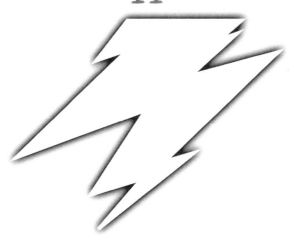

"Here he comes!" whispered Sean. "Give me the torch and get ready to run."

Mr Evans began to sneak up the driveway, trying hard not to make too much noise. Somewhere in the distance a dog howled, adding to the spooky feel of the dark night.

"*Yoo-hoo*," called Sean in a high voice, sounding just like Mr Evans' wife.

Sean was very good at imitating other people's voices.

Then Rod, who was good at whistling, did a low wolf-whistle.

Mr Evans stopped walking.

Sean poked one arm out from around the side of the house and waved. "Over here, *Wil-bur*," he called again.

Mr Evans put down the petrol can and took a step forward. "Who's there?" he hissed. "Frances? Is that you?"

"Come and see what *I've* found," called Sean in a sing-song voice.

Stupid Mr Evans seemed to actually think that his wife had somehow got up to the farm, and that she was calling him. Leaving the petrol can in the middle of the drive, he began to run on tiptoe towards them.

"Quick!" whispered Sean.

The boys raced back the way they had come. Sean crouched behind the thunder box and Rod ran to the back door of the farmhouse, hiding in the shadows there.

"Wilbur, *heeelp meee*," cried Sean, his voice not sounding so good this time, because he was trying hard not to laugh.

Mr Evans came around the back of the house and stopped. Sean flashed his torch on and off. Mr Evans stepped forward again, although this time, more slowly. It looked as though he might have guessed he was being led into a trap. He was quite close to the thunder box now and Sean kept quiet, not wanting to scare him away.

"I see you, you little brat," Mr Evans hissed, running forward and making a grab for Sean. "Thought you'd trick me, did you? Wait 'till I get my hands on you!"

Sean scuttled out from behind the thunder box and began to run in circles around it. Mr Evans was close behind, desperately trying to grab hold of him. Then suddenly, the door of the thunder box flew open, all by itself. Mr Evans ran straight into it, hitting his head.

"Ouch!" he cried, falling backwards into the thunder box.

Rod switched an outdoor light on and came running up. Together, he and Sean began to wind the long coil of rope around the thunder box. They tied it up so that Mr Evans could not escape.

"That was close," puffed Sean. "I thought he'd get me!"

Mr Evans began to hammer on the door. "When I get out, you're going to wish you were dead," he yelled.

"I hope this old toilet will hold him," worried Rod.

"I'm counting on it to take him for a spin and keep him occupied until the police get here," grinned Sean.

"Well, I'm not," said Rod. "You go and get the keys out of Mr Evans' car so he can't drive off if he gets out. I'm going to wake up Grandpa."

The boys ran off in different directions as the thunder box shook and rattled. Mr Evans was trying hard to kick and punch his way out.

A loud rumble sounded and a streak of blue lightning hit the thunder box with a sizzle. The little building lifted itself off the ground and spun in the air, flying crazily about, its wooden boards rattling. It landed in the cow paddock, bouncing along roughly before taking off again and flying over the roof of the farmhouse. Finally, it gave a tired groan and landed back beneath the pine tree.

"Grandpa! Grandpa! Wake up!" shouted Rod. "Mr Evans came up here with a can of petrol. He was going to burn the house down, but we've locked him in the thunder box!"

"What did you say, Rodney?" mumbled Grandpa Bill, sitting up in bed and rubbing his eyes. "Wilbur Evans wouldn't do such a thing."

"Come and see for yourself," insisted Rod, tugging at Grandpa's arm. "We have to call the police."

Sean arrived back at the thunder box with the key to Mr Evans' car in his hand, just as Rod was dragging Grandpa Bill outside. The thunder box was quiet. Its door sagged and it looked worn out.

"Is this a joke, boys?" asked Grandpa. "There's nobody in there!"

Rod and Sean looked at each other.

"Oh, no, he escaped!" exclaimed Rod.

"I don't think so," said Sean, holding up the key. "I think we got that help I was hoping for."

"What help?" asked Grandpa, getting really annoyed. "This is most unlike you, Rod. Fancy saying someone was trying to burn the house down. That's a terrible thing to say!"

"Grandpa, it's true!" declared Rod. "Come with us and we'll show you; there's a can of petrol in the middle of the driveway and Mr Evans' four-wheel drive is here. See – Sean has the key to it!"

Grandpa Bill looked at the key and then nodded his head. "Okay," he grumbled. "You'd better show me."

Rod's grandpa realised the boys were telling the truth when he saw the petrol and the four-wheel drive. "I never realised Wilbur wanted the place so badly," he muttered, shaking his head and going back inside to phone the police.

"Let's hope the thunder box goes and brings Mr Evans back at just the right time," Sean whispered to Rod.

"Don't count on it," replied his friend. "Mr Evans probably escaped, but the police will find him." And he went back inside to check on Grandpa Bill.

Chapter 7

Delivery

Sean stayed outside in the dark. He walked up to the thunder box and noticed that the rope had gone from around it. He took a peek inside. It was completely empty. Sean thought it was very strange that when people were taken away in the thunder box, the whole thing didn't lift off and disappear. And yet, when he rode in it, it seemed like the thunder box had travelled with him. He wondered how it worked. It was magic in some way – and very spooky. Suddenly the toilet-roll holder rattled and the thunder box did lift a little way off the ground, as if it were just showing Sean that it could! Blue lightning sizzled across its roof and a bubbling sound came from inside the toilet. Sean could have sworn that, for a moment, the thunder box was laughing. He quickly slammed the door and backed away.

Just then, a police car drove up with flashing lights. Sean hurried over to meet it.

"We heard a noise and we saw Mr Evans with the petrol can, whispering to himself that he was going to set the place on fire," Rod was explaining to two policemen, as Sean ran up. "We locked Mr Evans in the thunder box, but we think he escaped."

Rod sounded convincing and the policemen believed him. "You'd better show us, son," said one of them.

Everyone trooped around to the back of the house, once again. Sean hoped that the thunder box had got its timing right. Luckily, it had. A flicker of blue light was just disappearing from the roof as they approached.

"Hey! What am I doing in here with you, Evans?" asked a puzzled voice from inside. "I just got out of bed to go to the toilet, and now I find myself in this stinking hole!"

"How would I know?" they heard Mr Evans retort. "But I think it's only fair, since it was your idea for me to burn the farmhouse down in the first place!"

"I've heard enough," said one of the policemen, getting his handcuffs out.

The policemen threw open the thunder box door and quickly arrested Mr Evans and another man.

"Councillor Richardson!" gasped Grandpa Bill. "You were in on this, too?"

"I don't know what you're talking about, or how I got here," said a confused little man in pyjamas. "I was in bed just a few minutes ago."

"So we heard – you can do your explaining down at the station," the policeman gruffly told him as he snapped on the handcuffs. "How could you think of burning down this poor fellow's house?"

"What crooks!" exclaimed Grandpa Bill. "You saved my home, boys, and I've got a lot to thank you for. But how did you know what was going on – and how did Councillor Richardson get here?"

"Um … I'm not really sure," said Rod. "Perhaps Sean can explain."

Grandpa Bill looked at Sean. "Well, Sean?"

Sean looked back at the thunder box, remembering the lightning. "I think it's got something to do with the thunderstorms you've been having around here lately," he said. "When you and Rod were inside phoning the police, I saw something really weird."

"Perhaps you'd better tell me over a cup of hot chocolate," Grandpa Bill sighed.

43

Chapter 8

When Lightning Strikes ...

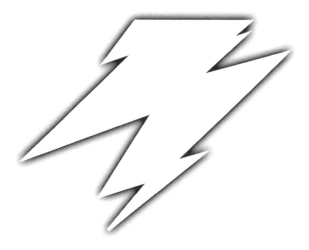

"You mean, you think the thunder box has come to life?" asked Grandpa Bill, after Sean had relayed the events and what he made of them. Grandpa Bill stared out of the kitchen window at the thunder box, and shivered.

Sean sipped at his chocolate and nodded. "You were right, Rod; it wasn't aliens. The thunder box has a mind of its own. It somehow found out Mr Evans wanted the farm, and it needed us to help stop him."

"I wondered about that," said Rod. "But I didn't want to say anything to you, because it sounded so silly."

"At first I thought it was a silly idea, too," said Sean. "But then I remembered the lightning and the thunderstorms around here. Do you remember our teacher telling us about the first life on Earth?"

Rod scratched his head. "No," he said.

"Well, I do," continued Sean. "Our teacher told us that scientists think the first life on Earth might have started billions of years ago, when lightning kept striking the sea. Stuff in the sea used the energy from lightning to make living things, so maybe the thunder box used the energy too."

"You're a clever boy, Sean," said Grandpa Bill. "I'm an old man and I've seen lots of strange things in my time, so I suspect you may be right. But – I don't think we'd better tell anyone else about this, do you?"

Rod and Sean shook their heads. "Nobody would believe us," sighed Rod.

● ● ●

The next morning, Grandpa Bill got up bright and early. He looked at the thunder box and thought about what Sean had said. Then he had an idea. He took a long metal rod from the barn and hammered it into the ground next to the thunder box, attaching it to the wall with a bit of wire.

"What are you doing, Grandpa?" asked the boys, coming out in their pyjamas to see what was going on.

"This is a lightning rod," explained Grandpa. "Now, when lightning strikes the thunder box it will go straight down the rod and into the ground where it belongs, instead of bringing my toilet to life! Electricity prefers metal, you see."

Rod and Sean looked at the thunder box

and felt rather sorry for it. "Will *all* its energy disappear?" asked Rod.

"I don't know," said Grandpa Bill. "But I hope so. Although it saved the farmhouse, I don't really want a thunder box with a mind of its own."

"Grandpa Bill, have you ever considered getting an *indoor* toilet?" asked Sean, as they all turned to walk back to the farmhouse for breakfast.

"I am now," laughed the old man. "I'm considering it very seriously!"

As soon as they had gone, the thunder box's door burst open and swung back and forth. Inside, the toilet-roll holder spun around. Then all was still ...

About the Author

Heather Hammonds lives with her family at the foot of the Dandenong Ranges, near Melbourne. She has written a number of stories about Rod and Sean and their wild adventures and, in her spare time, she enjoys exploring the Internet and walking her dog.

BlitzIt is here! Once you've read one **BlitzIt** book, you'll want to read them all.

Mystery ... adventure ... alien visitors ... weird science ... spooky happenings ... BlitzIt has something for everyone!

Set A:
Bargains from Outer Space
Birthday Surprise
Expiry Date
Hell-ectric Guitar
Monopillar
The Twins in the Trunk

Set B:
Monkey Business
School for Bad Kids
Sickle Moon Ghost
The Aitutaki Phantom
The Haunted Quilt
Thunder Box